Praise for *Chamiso*

"Amalio Madueño's *Lost in the Chamiso* follows in the great tradition of William Carlos Williams's *Paterson* and Charles Olson's *Maximus Poems*, and like those forerunners interweaves the personal with the historical and the mythical to create a rich fabric of the imagination.

With great good humor, seriousness and candor Madueño speaks from the inter-lingual borderlands that shape our future.

His vision and message are vital."

--Sam Hamill

"As a sister Yaqui Pocha, who now lives in San Miguel de Allende, Mexico (with the very poor Indians begging on the streets, to the wealthy who buy art that would support them for years), *Lost in the Chamiso* has reached me on the trade route winds.

The ancient trade routes that knew no human borders for centuries... Madueño reached me across the imaginary border of Mexico/USA."

--Alma Luz Villanueva

copyright 2006
book/cover design antoinette nora claypoole
cover photo "road to magdalena", antoinette nora claypoole

All rights revert to author. Small portions of this book (up to 10 pages)
can be used freely with proper credit given to author.
For extensive use of this book, please contact publisher.
Special arrangements provided to educational settings, art groups and artists.

Print acknowledgments:
Portions of *Lost in the Chamiso* previously appeared in:
Americas Review (Houston 1990), *Prairie Schooner* (Lawrence, KS, 1991), *Poetry* (Chicago, 1993), *Exquisite Corpse* (Baton Rouge 1997 print & Online), *Strong Coffee* (Chicago 1998), *Thus Spake the Corpse* (Baton Rouge 1999), *Suitcase* (UCLA, Los Angeles 1999), *The Temple* (WallaWalla, WA 2000), *Saludos: Poets of New Mexico* (2000 Pennywhistle Press , Santa Fe) *Familia* (Romania, 2001), *Chokecherries: Taos Poets* (Taos, 2001), *Rigor Mortis*,(El Paso, 2002, *Solo* (Ventura, 2003), *Sin Fronteras* (Las Cruces, New Mexico, 2003); *ArtLife* Magazine (Ventura, CA 2004), , *La Puerta, Taos: The Art of Fetching Sky* (Wild Embers Press, 2006).

First Printing, printed in the USA.
Wild Embers is committed to the Green Initiative
and is a member of the New Mexico Book Association

Wild Embers Press
po box 3026
ashland, or. 97520

www.wildembers.com
All People are One

Lost in the Chamiso

an epic poetic portale

by Amalio Madueño

Wild Embers   New Mexico

CONTENTS

Author's Notes
Pocho in the Linguistic Wilderness by Laurie Macrae
Introduction by Alma Luz Villanueva

Part One   ***Borderland***

Garcia's Experience 3
Tortillas 4
Freedom of the Press 6
Cruiser 8
Toxic Waste 9
Hourly Wages 11
Agriculture 13
Desaparecidos 16
Trucking 18
Middle Spring 19
Questions 20

Part Two *Lost in the Chamiso*

How Old Am I 25
The Water 26
The Crossing 27
The Colonia as Social Structure 30
Snow Storm Blankets El Chuco 31
Lost in the Chamsio 32
Drug Lord 33
US 34
Border Pecans 35

Part Three *Coyote Observes Humans*
My Dead Abuelitas 39
Coyote Observes Humans 40
Everyone is Part Yaqui 42
Pocho Deer Song 46
Garcia's Walking Pharmacopoeia Blues 49
Menudo 52
Regador 54
Cook Up Some Pork Chops 56
Death of a Soldier 58
Song X 60
Casino 61
Day of the Dead 62
Nogal 64
Winter Dance 65
Hand Dance 66
Whirling Disease 66
Horse Eats Man 67

Part Four ***El Mirador***
The View From Here 71
Giant Screen 72
Menopause Motel 73
Principle of the Moon 74
The Love of Garcia 77
My Cemetery 78
Travelling Circus in Española 80
Astronomer Garcia 82
Expression Three 83
Garcia Walks 85
Garcia Builds A House 87
Hombre in the Moon 89
Real Experience 91
Laughs 93
Ordinary Pieces 96

Part Five *Garcia in Gringolandia*
Funebre en Amalia 100
San Ysidro 55 104
Garcia in Gringolandia 106
Garcia's Luz Especiale 107
Garcia's Dog Poem 108
Garcia Prepares for Winter 110
Rollergirl 111
Garcia Meets the Holy Bitch 112

Author's Notes

Lost in the Chamiso is a woven compendium of chapbooks--poetry written between 1997 and 2005—while performing and recording poetry in New Mexico and the Southwest (plus some extras that never got into print). I wrote them in the context of an intense period of interaction with a varied Southwest/Border audience infused with Tex-Mex, Anglo, Native American, Migrant, Chicano and student listeners. Audiences for my poetry took many forms, from the staid and circumspect academic seminar full of El Paso or Taos college students and professors, to raucous beer & smoke soaked North vs. South poetry bouts at El Patio Bar in Mesilla, to Santa Fe gallery-staged jazz-accompanied white wine exhibitions.

Every performance was an attempt to "make it new" and provide poetry that created a poetic environment true to my sensibility, which is Mexican-American and Border-oriented with strong notes of Spanglish, desert landscape and sweaty work. *Chamiso* reflects those discreet time periods of unique Poetry Circus Mexican-Bob experience–somewhat like annual vintages.

This collection becomes, now, a "poetic epic" through Wild Embers editor, antoinette claypoole. Suggesting a shake up of the linear progression, antoinette placed the original poems of *The God of this Vicinity* into italics, wove them throughout the book, and created, as she explains, "an epic and emergent voice-- a thread of story within the story--whispers beyond/into time."

And, since one can't really ever get lost in the chamiso
(a three foot tall high desert shrub)
enjoy.

Amalio Madueño
Taos, N.M. June 5, 2006

Acknowledgements

Thanks to antoinette claypoole, Paul Nelson & Charles Potts for their excellent and collegial comraderie, my *compadres de poesia* during the years this work was written.

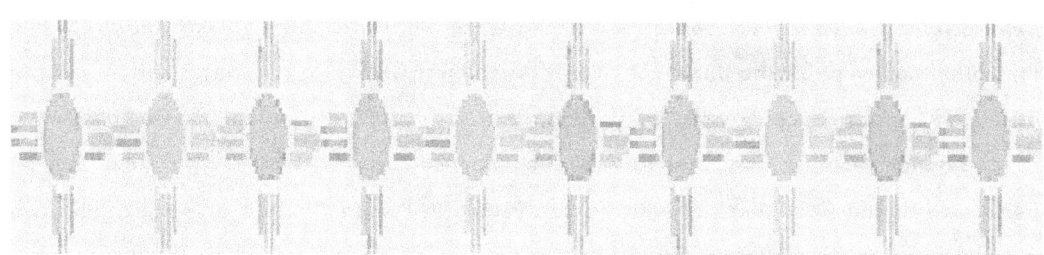

to Pablito, Tsunami and Reina Rosa

Pocho in the Linguistic Wilderness

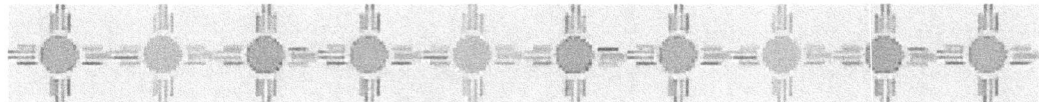

The poetry of Amalio Madueño uses the language of the American Southwest border regions. Sometimes called Chicano Spanish, it is the constantly changing idiomatic expression of a culture within a culture, a "mental/spiritual non-country" as described by Francisco Lomeli. Some words like "pocho" (an Americanized Mexican or Hispanic) have a distinctly pejorative connotation which reflects the strong sense of cultural identity within the area, and the coded contempt for the dominant culture. Madueños work also references certain cultural events and performances specific to the Southwest, such as the Matachines dances performed in traditional Hispanic and Native American communities, and the Yaqui Deer Dance, performed during Holy Week at New Pascua Pueblo in Tucson. These events have their own cultural meaning, and much of the related nomenclature is familiar only to those who have witnessed and/or studied them, or who are members of the indigenous community that performs them. In many instances a rudimentary familiarity with Spanish will probably suffice to make the most necessary connections, as the poet does not strive for obscurity, but rather to transform and expand our notions of interethnic relations.

Laurie Macrae
San Diego Public Library, 2001
San Diego, California

For additional assistance, **The Dictionary of Chicano Spanish** by Roberto Galvan
and Richard V. Teschner [NTC 1981] is an excellent resource,
as is **The Matachines Dance** by Sylvia Rodriguez
[UNM Press 1996] for translating vocabulary and significant cultural events.

Introduction

Lost in the Chamiso is a tidal wave of words, images, experiences, joy, anger, humor, great sorrow, great ecstasy, stories leaping from page to page in the 'five parts' of this epic poem. He writes, sings, and remembers. Amalio Madueño reaches to Juarez, Mexico, to the women in black mourning the desparecidas, the young women who've 'disappeared'...in ten years, 400 young women...
They disappear and then we find them," he tells us.
Further on is the story of his Tia Lalo who was told by a white woman during the depression: "No wetback should have shoes like that in times like this!"

Madueño writes of assimilation of the 50s (*I remember this well, when as a young girl I was punished for speaking Spanish- my first language- at school*). In the poem, *How Old Am I*, he insists: "Remember and mind and remember" Exactly, this is it- do not disappear, do not assimilate, and DO wear those shiny new shoes that love to dance. He reminds us: "The most important thing is transformation," and that's what these poems do- all five parts- they are in constant transformation, to remember and mind and remember, to transform.

We are revived in the poem, *Pocho Deer Song, After The Yaqui Traditional*
as Madueño sings:
I am a Pocho alive in the fantastic wilderness...
It is still going on, the wilderness still listens,
Listens to itself- even now.

ALMA LUZ VILLANUEVA
May 20, 2006
San Miguel de Allende, Mexico

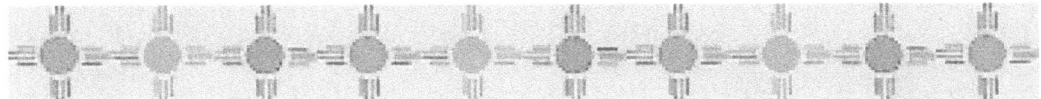

Song on a Jemez Wind

Teakettle sings to me
Ancient kiva hymn
Granite throat notes
Battleground moans
Blood drenched sand whine
A voice over stretched wire
Like joy fathering lip and tongue
Working proving time
Does not simply move to the beat
Like the drum when it is wet
As the beat of it trips my hands
As a bird near the river's edge
Makes every effort to cut a flow
Stop a clock peel a flash
Air folds slipknots
Tied to the wind's satisfaction

Part one

Borderland

His mother was a green bouquet of kelp. She bore him over a period of three days down by the shipyard. The harbor was a flotsammed, jagged place for an alien kid to play. He ignored the many just like him trying to find a way to shallows, sandbars, and shoals. On the silver strand, he noticed how the shorebirds skimmed for succulent tips and spears as they cruised the crashing waves, the spreading spume and foam.

Garcia's Experience

Garcia's experience in a lot of areas
Allows him to fit into almost any job
And look good at it. Starting young
His mother taught him to sew, knit, and put
On appearances. Self-taught in mind
Control and ideas not hard to come by
He has worked *toda su vida* in all manner
Of *jale* with attention to detail and results:
Restaurant work dishes prep cook lifeguard
Legislative consultant fish cannery in Puerto
Penyasco *carpintero* to the stars remodeler
Handyman has been self-employed in cement
Foundations tunnels conduits gran boulevards
Bank consortiums mechanic forest service
Fire crew brush disposal unit pre-commercial thinning
Camp ground maintenance fish hunt
Minor plumbing some electrical traveled
The hemisphere in semis flatbeds some dump truck
Crewed 36-passenger fantasy ship
1,000 units of low-income housing
Part of his ability is he can always
See another way to manage reality
Raised on .3 acres of hardpan
Suburban postage stamp his dad made
Sure he knew assimilation crushed
The juice out of him to the ground
That feeding horses chickens dogs and cats
A pet rat was just not in the cards
Had only an inkling of the old ways
Deciphered the long honk of a Ford better
Than the lone cry of a wading bird
Can go anywhere and be OK
                      In almost any situation

She becomes dizzy at the sight of orchids. Her sons turn pale at the sight of their own juice. La reina telectronica cannot control the vibrations she gets from border patrol officers. All her ancestors can drink a pint of cahuama blood at one sitting. They keep a pot of menudo simmering all night, every night, chopping cebolla & cilantro, crushing red chile, flipping giant tortillas on fired-up 50 gallon drums. The traffic roars. A trogon talks convincingly to her from deep in the arroyo. Eventually, she no longer wakes up trailing dreams of the bosque.

Tortillas

I
God is a kilo of steaming tortillas that does nothing
      but make a sphere of aroma.
I've studied the ancestry of corn, sought out the madre de maiz,
      chewed the juice of teosinte.
It is on no page in any tome, finds
      no place on any page
Given this reality the *princessas*, the *jovenitas*,
      the *viejitas* churning out,
Patting out, cranking tortillas forever look
      very important, very serious.
No *Ave Marias* prayed to heaven solve the mystery,
      save me from tilling rows,
Hauling water, squashing the worms, spraying
      the fungus, driving the dusty
Afternoons of August wildly to the horizon.

II
I unfold the wrapping and think:
I've eaten more tortillas than anyone I know
Hot cold rolled flat fried steamed flamed burnt
Plain or with butter baloney salami tuna
        peanut butter salsa guacamole
Walking out of the tortillaria in Tijuana
Put your nose to the wrapping paper
Forget the corn shortage, the field where it grows
October corn November corn December corn
Steamy tortillerias con 2-ton maquinas @ 1,000 btu.
Streams of tortillas at 100 per minute
        What do they cost a penny or two

III

In a festive plaza humming with music I dance
In my tortilla suit I dance and dance. It's a special day,
A feast day with abundance and variety, a celebration
For a single goddess moving amongst the crowd.
The only hint of her presence -- corn silk here and there
Glistening in the sunlit breeze, in this dance
Where sun, mountain, river and goddess are one.
A tetradic deity I must honor in careful movements
Timed to meet each drumbeat in midair.
Each movement: hand, arm, head, bonnet, mask
Can only be understood in four ways, every minute,
Every hour all day for all to witness and understand.
At sunset I lie down surrounded by leaves
And watch the stars appear one by one with her.
Kernels of light awaiting the moon to devour them.

Freedom of the Press

Early morning hours and Robert Mora García,
Editor of *El Mañana,* is *muerto* outside mi casa,
Police radio-crackle surrounds me
As I watch his oozing wounds and remember
Shots outside my dawn-blue windows.
Mi casa es su casa. The phrase sinks down,
Weighted with what I've seen. Who will say
Along with me, "*mis casa es su casa*"?
Who will smooth his dusty hair?
There isn't much the *madrugada* patrol
Can do, in any case. Mora, dead outside
With nothing left to write about,
As the day grows, as the wounds ooze,
There is this much else to add
        Shuffling noises, radio-crackle, mixed
        mañana sounds, clustered, clotted, A wallet
        With 20 pesos ($2 U.S.) lying there
        Cell phone in his pantalones ringing
        La Cucaracha, ringing, tatata-Ta-TA!
        Keys in the ignition, driver door open
        window rolled down . . .
Outside his casa, mi casa, all morning
Clouds have been sliding out of the Gulf
All night dust stirred in the *paseo*, shifting
Its weight, and now the day begins to sear.
Tiny points of heat pierce even
The deepest patios of mi casa, su casa.

She often got lost somewhere in the chaparral.

*Her father would find her entwined in pungent chamisal.
She would get lost again and again deep in Arroyo Seco… on purpose. On moonlit nights she filled her pockets with balls from the far end of the driving range.*

Sometimes she was home watching the clock, turning the channel, flipping the page.
Other times, she sat at the base of a cedar cracking piñon with her white front teeth.

While she followed her father delivering mail, whistling along infinite pavements,
a striped blue lizard looked for her in the underbrush,
flicking his speedy tongue in every corner.

Cruiser

Cruise, niño, cruise,
Francisco Javier Reza Pacheco's
Juárez Cruiser Crackdown
impounded eighty cars mijo,
y quien s'ai bruised bodies

Reza Pacheco detects & fines
cruisers drag & race,
watchale niño for Pacheco!
adults caught seep and bleed
serve 36 hours, mijo!

18 or younger al Systema
with bandages, major injuries
and minor tickets mijo

wachale! under over around
city street rehab,
Under & around Pacheco's
funny face, cruise, mijo, cruise!

Toxic Waste

The reason for toxicity in the lagoon
Is a double chain chemical compound,
A form of viscous liquid similar to burned oil
400 barrels in our own front yard
Immersed and sealed in cement and somebody
Found it and somebody touched it and now we're all hurting

I would rather raise a victory cry celebrating
The end of construction -- a day so happy the mist
Lifts from the lagoon with hummingbirds
And there is nothing in the world I covet,
And all the injury I have known is gone
And knowing it has taken so long to be certain of some
Small important things about the world does not pain me,
And in this landscape I feel completely at home
While I dive headfirst with arms outstretched.

La Tiendita is a tiny store out in the flats specializing in eggs and beer and such. Garcia goes around with a feather duster, fly swatter, and goggles. Taz! Taz! No flyspecks on the Tecate! Get away from my blanquillas! No brats near the Cuervo miniatures! Painted mouse skulls dangle from the walk-in fridge. A large mosca plops on a pearly egg. G makes a grimace and his lips clench. On his head he wears a fake deer head with tiny antlers tied on with scarlet ribbon.

Hourly Wages

All I want is flexible hours
dynamic, bilingual bendable hours
individual hours queued for miles
into the desert emerging Hispano
Euro market hours Mexican
hours in any language hours
joined to mine with infinite filaments
support hours intoned in spanish
& french hours & hours of independence
ability hours buzzing & fluttering
position hours available now
offering hours competing for attention
benefit hours langorous & yearning
flexible hours, immensely flexible
bending and turning for me

Garcia pressing her hotly with his oiled and decorated fingers. She slips one hand around him as if he were a child that needed urging. The moan she uses is like the single note in his blood, but the timbre is hers entirely. "You might give me greater pleasure with a different approach," she opines. She's right, he thinks.

Always, since he's been sinking in her steam, there has been this quaking certainty. His chilly room has been known to disappear entirely in vaporous night.

Agriculture

Everyone wants a part of me.
Its making me a loco!
There's the *chileros* from el Norte,
then the *chileros* from el Sur,
the hermanos y hermanas,
the padres from Sierra Tarahumara
brought by international programs,
the *meztizos* and *gente indigena* who
have no clue what they are in for . . .
It's the *americanos,* tonto!
Here to take you from yourselves!
Corn kilos, sheep, goats, chickens
cattlemen dumping clean herds,
30 meters of federal Red Tape
Innocuous sub-frozen inoculum
for Fed verification studies,
Y, an FDA guy with a food label law . . .
like I says: meat quality and
diet and stress and pork . . .
gee does my life count?
Lengua brings it all together...
do you know where E*l Rincon* is?
yes its down the street, at the corner!
Great name for a bar, *que no*?

Granpo was so rich he never paid for anything. All alone on Black Mesa in his half-pipe Silverstream, he would drink gin and eat candy bars, waiting for the hookers to arrive. Y volver, volver, volver . . . G never heard him sing. Instead, there was mostly silence. His mother cut up the mink stole Granpo gave her to make him a Davy Crockett hat before she went out to commit grand larceny.

Reina considers herself the first in a line of consultant warriors. It's been no time at all since she put on her warrior socks and stalked into government offices to wreak havoc among the ignorantes. The roads are lined with the charred hulks of those who did not heed her counsel. The Cyclopean forest ranger wants to achieve sustainable biomass, and R has nothing to suggest to him. "The bosquistas are claiming Truchas y Vallecitos!" R declaims in La Mesilla. "The Tejanos are yodeling still about all that timber they bought, their humvees crashing through the forest flora!"

In a brief respite, she neatly places chunks of copal in a ceremonial brazier and inhales thick wisps of smoke through her large nostrils.

Desaparecidas

They disappear and then we find them
The reason the women of Júarez wear black
The reason for the *gritos* citations and web links
About 10 years and 400 women
Young sexual bodies *autoridades* dismiss

They disappear and then we find them
The reason mothers of the dead wear black
The reason for perpetual funeral marches
The reason they walk silent with black crosses

 They disappear and then we find them
17 since August their mothers place candles
cards names dates they were killed

They disappear and then we find them
The reason for crucifixes spread before
The Palacio del Gobierno's traffic and noise
17 per month in Buendia colonia
24 in Cuidad Centro 97 in four years.

They disappear and then we find them
Their last moments diaphanous facts
Adrift in papers and trash on Avenida Revolucion

                                        They disappear and then we find them

It was the fifties – the time of the Great Assimilation. Some evenings she understood how everyone in the country had the same thought balloon floating above his head. She knew it was a form of thinking -- each balloon wavering on its tether, tinged with intimations of catastrophe, the velocity of extinction.

"We would think incessantly," she remembered, "breathless with conformity. Later, we'd comment on the lack of coherence, the way the certainty of the young was inspiring and frightening at once. In the morning there was cereal & milk while cocky disk jockeys massaged the airwaves. TV commercials blared at each housewife deaf behind her vacuum."

Trucking

The first bug of Spring hit the windshield
And the horizon out past the Chiricahuas
Was a pale slice of watermelon
I had a truck full of flagstone
Dug from a road cut near *el sanctuario*
And I was happy-tired looking forward
To some downtime when I felt it
Like I was driving through a new world
Without having left the old, then
Some lightning touched the ground out west
While the engine ate up the miles heading south

Thirty years after the end of the season, he showed up. He had changed. No more football uniform, cleats worn to stipples, cobwebs in the earholes of his helmet. Bronze muscles no longer rippled under shiny spandex. He still carried the famous ball that penetrated any zone, but the laces were gone. Whatever the image, he held no frisson for us. "Hechale compañero!" we shouted as he faked and feinted his way up the alley.

Middle Spring

Below me and above, middle Spring.
Blossom air soothes gravel and stone.
Birds in my shaggy yard scamper in dust
At home in morning's ocean breeze.
Night after night dreams become less
Familiar, like the landscape of a city
I will never see. Today is light,
Tomorrow will be lighter still. Sundogs
Streak the perihelion, spiders drop
Filaments of light out of the blue
Into sunny scrutiny – the intersection
Of the everyday.

Questions

The questions will be there in the morning
Holding on all night until the light returns
The word *damage* reaches mind, and I consider it
As I watch traffic snarl and smolder in the interchange.
All that tonnage sinking into pavement
Weighted with oils of ecstasy and sorrow.
No one will swerve, no one will lean on the horn,
Lay on the brights to catch a glimpse as they skid
By in the glare and confusion of dusk and rush hour.
Side-lit, flash-panned they spin away
Like pinballs wherever a void appears,
Fluid, jack-braking, multi-lingual in their own noise
All evening red lights slide toward the coast
All evening bright halogens burn holes
Through the canopy of decision. And now
They are upon us, specks of uncertainty streaming
In a bright rain right at us.

"You remember the story about me and the uppity white girl," says Tia Lola. "It was the Depression; she goaded me about my new leather shoes." 'No wetback should have shoes like that in times like this!' she told me. My father gave me a hatpin to defend myself. After our next encounter, she never came to school again."

part two

Lost in the Chamiso

The desert was no longer alive. He crawled through a hole gnawed long ago by giant ants. The rising sun glinted on the stubble of catastrophe. "I imagine," Garcia said, "how in a future time one might devolve to a form of agave azul tequilana, sending down roots to drink." [1]

How Old Am I

My memories fade like daybreak stars
Once brilliant in mind's dark
In the wide blue void not a hook
A line, or a sinker -- only a raven swooping
The ash heap, honking geese heading north
Ragged snow clouds on Gallegos Peak
Grip fading on a cherished bundle
Another drag and back to dreams
Running with the winds in another world
Forever fastened by filament and fetch
Wind scours gnarled roots
Portale echoes grind adobe and pine
Remember and mind and remember

GARCIA APPEARS NIGHTLY:
Out back of The Void--A Wood-Fired Pizzeria
Wilted lechuga in a white plastic bucket
Under a clothesline draped with meat.

The Water

Always attracted to surface and horizon --
The deeper than here hemisphere's blue.
Light shards boomerang, broken
From angled sun as I drift like a barge.
Moment to moment I become more liquid,
Flow with a current high to low,
Ending in the continental trench
Dusk splintered by water lights, pulls
Keening birds on amber lanes
Down to a rushing tide

The nopal is a succulent with attitude.
Everything in it can be used for moistening.
And something else, Garcia thinks:
Your moisture or its moisture, what's the difference? In the sizzling arroyo,
your shadowy guts naturally quiet down, like a lizard under a rock.

The Crossing

The crossing roars like the shore in storm surf
It is high noon and desire, like a hawk, hovers
Over idling traffic. And it will swoop, believe me.
Up north the freeway begins its long exhalation.
Off ramps spool out to the horizon
High noon is bleeding all over the polished ocean
High noon folds the power poles into origami
High noon raises a dust up and blankets
The foothills with smog, desire wings its way
Through the hazy distance. Can we keep it
In sight? Can we call it back, give it a glove to find?
Or should we let it disappear in commercial flightpaths
Should we turn back to calculating our worth,
The value of our transactions? The passing through,
The collecting, the fee, the constant fee.

Reina Rosa's shiny black hair is spiked fashionably, the more to signify her lust for life in the narrow hallways of the mundane. Bureaucrats call her la femme d'affaires but she pays them no heed. She keeps her eyes wide open. Her meek assistants turn their heads away when she speaks, sweating tiny beads. Garcia hears it all from one of her reputed lovers, a bearded old goat, well-hung, who insists he's been doing her daily, discreetly, for years in her private rooms.

"She still comes like an earthquake," he says.

Garcia took in the homeless -- a gardener-poet, the infirm primo, wandering Tarahumaras. The ruca loca in tight skirt and halter-top did his weekly ironing with rollers in her hair, humming la Macarena. Her name was Chavela from Zacatecas. She kept to the Holy Word, inspired by mescal and lengua antigua. She insisted G was condenado even before the age of innocence.

She dragged his foto door to door evangelizing, demonstrating how indelible was his original sin, "even with Baptism & Communion," she said.

The *Colonia* As Social Structure

Colonia border shanty homes
from recycled materials,
amidst every obstacle a view
from within that has no voice
Texas, New Mexico Califas
little *colonia* big *colonia*
no view beyond within
Mud and dirt slum rental
permanent migrations in one place
mystifying mutating formations
the kind of thinking that leads
to no small problem
a view from within without a voice
marginal beyond reach
the view has no beyond or within
pockets of chronic natural disaster
forms of diseased view
without voice beyond or within
vacuums created by material fetish
views from within without voice
vacuum views that fly doomed

Snow Storm Blankets El Chuco

Sub-zero snow falls on the border
Snow paralyzing the metroplex
Record-breaking cold more severe even than
The mountains. Surely it caused the deaths –
Exposure and gas fumes from heaters – though
They prepared themselves as if they were warned.
Serious, even tragic, poor things, one would say
They heard neither the song of the north, nor
The secret whispers of the clouds. Likewise
They seem not to have seen what was plain
And common to all of us with television.
They must have been ignorant, and in their voids
They came to grief. All their expressions died
In their eyes, and lost themselves to a simple lowering
Of the temperature, to a shadow. Since there is little of
The north in them – nothing in their skin or their sunny
Fragile minds but warmth, love and sincerity, it was
Impossible for them to put themselves into
Positions that were obstinate, ardent, secure, required.
They have a kind of forlornness now, a rigid grace
And this will follow them to the barren cemeteries
Of Juarez, blowing dust and empty at sundown
Of desire, love, jealousy, dusts that scatter
And rise and fall on Avenida Revolution as the lights
Flash and cars honk and the troubled walk the streets
Like furry stones burning their way through

Thinker of infinite mathematique with your spirit toys, I'm listening. I'm listening. Show me your titanium-molybdenum prototype heart with its secret chambers. Watch it pump and sigh on the mahogany desk. I know there's a market for it. But a qualified manufacturer? Art. Toy. Jewel. Light. Platonic Form. Maschinen-werkzeugteknik links are needed -- some inspired tool & die fool so spiritual he has only one purpose, and that is fading fast in the crush of time.

Lost in the Chamiso

I keep a box of things I've found in dreams:
A black stone, unbending wood,
Gnarly root and summoned bee, a snapshot
Of me in dog form, a door handle from the speeding car
I stopped with a glob of spit.

I pray hard for these things to remain
Like the dreams they rode in on
I pray for myself to remain here, even if I
Must suffer. I know how to suffer, can take a beating.
Go ahead, take me down, kick until the nose loosens
And the lip shreds. Go ahead, betray me after years
Of devotion and love. My power varies but I'll still
Look you in the eye, chase you down the arroyo,
Confront you with the truth you won't believe.

I know this is heaven, I dance a chaconne with the girl
Of my dreams in this heaven. Descended from trout,
Fish tattoos run from my medula to my ass in this heaven.
In this heaven I make my own shoes so I can walk
To my headstone on Red Mesa. Those who will join me
Are not easy to find:
>When I burn chamiso to thick black smoke
>When I plant and sing a song on a clear day
>When *verduras* are knee high at my arroyo party
>When I hold a driving ceremony by the roadside

I want to be in a trance. When I'm possessed, the spirit
Has a powerful appetite. When I'm possessed and must,
Nevertheless, go to work, I pour tequila down my throat
I'm halfway to being a spirit myself. I can appear
Mysteriously at just the right moment.
In this heaven, wine is just the beginning.

Drug Lord

Control the city says Mr. Vigil
Drug Lords fight for control
Each region moves drugs
Valuable drugs move constantly
Murder crews move it & move it
Criminal crews control the moves
Says Officer Vigil, Special Agent in Charge

Agent in charge of What?
My drugs move through regions
Past borders between links of Arriba and Baja
Between seeping bandages and clotting wounds
A region of where of what of why
Fight me for control Mr. Vigil
My drugs my moves my control
Agent in charge in charge of what?
Of *direccion?* Of north of south, of drugs?
The region between the sidewalk & the driveway?
Cheap drugs by the ton
Moving fast and hungry
In the evening of where & what & why
And I will be fed, prowling by myself in silence
Hanging out in chain link shadow
A flag of desire stuck to the fence
I'll gather it all and will not stop
Suck the money into the blank spaces
Blow the smoke into your eyes
Lick each breast with my blue tongue
You will allow this and greet me
With the hollows of your limbs
With the chambers of your hearts
With your pink, educated tongues
Clapping your hands and dancing
Offering me an honored place
Think about that, Agent Vigil,
Agent in charge

US

Our burden is the border, *la linea, la migra*
The Gringo's is the assumed cliché of a dominant culture
Our burden seems heavy to us
Some of us console ourselves with the idea that the maguey
        takes one hundred years to flower
Who knows
We Pochos, like everyone else, are deformed by our civilization
We are the mestizos
The ones leaping the fence
The zoot-suited money-laundering narco-capitalists
The religious superstitious childish mojados
The ignorant seething devious unpredictable wirejumpers
We're the ones with jobs with advanced degrees with cash
        With added value with panache
We're the Zapatista Comandante Democracy fiends
We are the ones who pick the peach
The ones sprayed daily with pesticide
The Guadalajara singing
Guitar plucking tequila guzzling cactus eaters
The *colonia* squatters the parachuters
The graffiti-crazed macho caballero low riders
The hurricane punching machines
The mural painting gold hammering mambo kings
The *sabios* the *fariseos* the *curanderos* the *maestros*
The *matachines* the *pascolas* the *sierpas* the *coludos*
The *juzgados* let out of jail free
We are the mongolian-celtic-ethiopian-apache
Complainers intoxicated by liberty

The fleas on the border all feed on Garcia's sweaty fatigue. That is how they survive: the coyote ferries them from alien to alien, then the Border Patrol shakes them out at the detention center for another go round in el taconito.

At night, east of Hachita they listen to the vigilantes and narcotraficantes . . . the season is so long they must lay their eggs ala brava wherever and whenever they can and never get to count them.

"Duro, this blood-sucking life," they whine to each other, and it's time to leap skyward once again, con alma, con gusto.

Border Pecans

The trees came from the east through the County
Agent. We lived under them and the moon cast
Shadows moving with us at night past
Storage sheds and tractor wheels, the river
Gurgling through the valley, descents into
Arroyos under agave blooms. Past it all,
Past all the border crossings, all the trails, the
Water bottles, the cold sandwiches, the idling
Vans in the outback, breathing in, breathing out.
O Mexico, we knelt and kissed the earth then.
A coyote trotted the yucca covered llano
And moths swarmed their stalks heavy with sex
Amid fields of chile and cotton, pecans step-children.
Desert species crawling at our doors and windows
And in a summer rainstorm in Mesilla running
Through the calabasa and chile to the shed, laughing.
The heat rose at dawn by Viejas Peak where a trogon
Fluttered in the crown of a silver cedar.
I looked at the campesinos, their brimming boxes in the
Green rows stretching to Black Mesa
As the day turned, the *cosecha* had begun once again.

Part Three

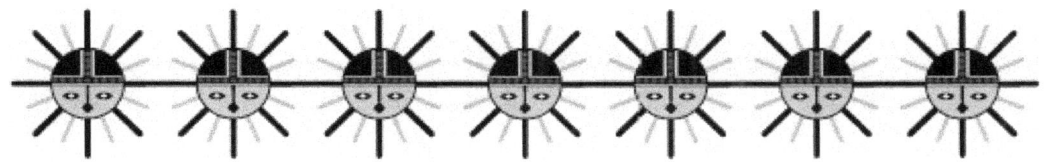

Coyote Observes Humans

Flashing '87 VW hood ornament on black lacquer, half-buried in hot arroyo sand. Garcia would like to know. Did they drive it down into the canyon side, kicking down loose sand, filling the back seat? He imagines other scenarios . . . It's been buried so long the finish is rusted out, the chrome is on its last millimeter. In the noon sun, he sees himself driving it, top down, into the wind.

My Dead Abuelitas

I thank my dead abuelitas while driving
Thank them both when alone on the highway
When I sense their care in snowshreds
Streaking an iced arroyo, their cold observance
From a feathered ridgeline of dormant encino
Their admonition in distant windshield flash
When the grasp at emptiness becomes a feast
When the solution of dream's puzzle makes me smile
In small roadside confessions I thank them
Watching over me and my skimpy prayers

Coyote Observes Humans

> *"Once a coyote always a coyote"*
> – Nora Naranjo Morse

Paradoxical, hybrid, borderland characters that you are,
Psychohistorical beings with penetrating eyes.

There is a truism that humans transcend earth
And sky, that they express the universal.
It is said they come from nowhere.

Coyotes are about little else than howling and hunting.
We merely express how we are in a song of the land.
Yet everywhere we are viewed with inescapable meaning.

Our dilemma is empirically inseparable from
The problem of humans. Classification of *fine*
Coyote and *folk* coyote --*folk* coyote
And *fine* -- dogs us to the steel traps.

Paradoxical, hybrid borderland characters that we are,
Psychohistorical *luminosos* with penetrating eyes.

Can we be truly *fine* coyotes only
In a mystified landscape devoid of humans? Can we
Be truly *folk* coyotes only in a laughing circle?
Must we let our ears and noses be
Appropriated *qualquiere* by those hungry for coyote sign?

Some of us put frills on our minds by
Self-consciously highlighting our mystery,
Our ability to cackle hysterically.
We compete in the pool of humans who exploit and proliferate
Turquoise notes and gewgaws.

Paradoxical, hybrid, borderland characters that we are,
Psychohistorical humans with penetrating eyes.
We are politicized native coyotes. We understand
That a thousand years is the only acceptable unit
Of political time. What is wrong with us
Is that we are constantly thinking about the wilderness
While most of you are thinking about hotcold
Wetdryblackwhitegainloss, indifferent and hostile
To the long term song of the land. We must be
More *coyotero* than ever before, must seize
The blackened heart from the fire and transform its meaning

Paradoxical, recondite, borderland characters that we are,
Pyschohistorical beings with nowhere eyes.

Garcia, lost in his own experiment, studying the manual on how to build the machine that builds the machine. A machine that runs on random amid bursts of sinister. The machine that makes the book that writes itself. Its index instructs radiant serifs between leaves of silhouette oak, reverse transcript of most common utterance return ticket to llano de nada ningun whose paragraph is lines of blue chamiso where ancient malediction's muscled hulk sulks below the blossom line. For every asterisk, a mouthful of anno sails the light dream edge of the word.

Everyone Is Part Yaqui

I
So last year the *chones* hung from their ears
Marching *fariseos* clacked their swords
At the goddess teetering on the dais
We came to see the flower people
Whacking away at evil between the trash barrels
Wedged there with clowns behind the vestibule
Flipping chairs in tortilla smoke
And slept where hungry spirits slithered
Tearing tiny holes in our clothes where
We turned in the hot dust to Guadalupe

I was fasting but had an iced *horchata*
While the rest chowed on *tacos al carbon*
We went to see where Chavez fought the priest
Where moonlight bloom agaves bowed
Under constellations afloat in traffic neon
We saw the cathedral, a Mediterranean sajuaro dream
With blood and fire murals over Indio-Catholic bricks
Now with speaker phone tours & gift shop

The *sabio* Conibomea sent two women
To Sinaloa in 1617 where they wandered among
Ocoronis and Guasaves inspecting Jesuit improvements
Nothing endures of the peace they crafted
Sands shift under creosote, cliffs erode
Teeming cities are reduced to chaos and violence
It was midnight on Good Friday
The hot dust had cooled to dry freshness
Pascuaros tuned their blood in murmurs
Outside the chapel knowing how the next
Day's light would sear their souls

Matachines bobbed and weaved in silence
    We are the blood choir
    Look to the heavens
    Starry night spins out
    The sparkling image of our fate

II
You could see little in the face of the wind
The brittle embers splashed against adobes
And shadow gestures of arms lengthened
In the shifting earth across the houseyard
Indecipherable as the dance I witnessed
Ending up at a point still further south
Of those Peloncillos already half worn
By steel radials and aeons of devout processions
Sacrificial fusion prayers complicated yet smooth
Like stele perhaps or like the trogon's plumage
Disappearing into a wilderness half forgotten
Yet still listening to itself and recognizable after all
In the face of that wind and from then on legs
Encrusted with earth and firelight reminded me
This is the time when we who make so much
Of being young must listen again in amazement
Finding ourselves older and needing a talking stick
More than requited love or goals achieved
Not knowing where else to look or how and I raised
The subject of the comet having moved from just below
Arcturus to the other horizon and the moon riding
A Pegasus cloud when the clacking swords again
Stopped our whispering and we sank into another state
Surprised at the good fortune accreting in the struggle with suffering
Behind us the popping flag the bell on a frayed rope
Sand-whipped symbols in acrylic blue glow on a cross
About to transform and I could hear them marching

In that wind as I wrapped myself closer to the pillars
Turning away to where the only explanations
Were mine and I heard their insistence their determination
To complete the fragrant battle in that whirling
The pulsating coals smelled of iron behind
Blue percale *munecas* staid in their nichos
Of dirt while the white lacework bier absorbed
Dumb looks from those like me still afraid to speak

III
Nothing was clear yet everything had a certain familiarity
We could only agree on the matter of seeing
And each had the sharp affinity that came with seeing more

We were going through the same country – immense
Terrestrial waves in shimmered mirage
Black damask silhouettes in orange dusk
Readable signals of how we thought about the god
The dance and the hill of the rooster reached us
In our jackets under the bell tower

Conch calls spilled my chocolate heart in the dirt
One rooted certainty in the witching dark
In early April we listened for the humming soul in the deer song
Nothing is false, we agreed, laughing
When these things happen they take the darkness out of time
Then I picked a yellow nopal blossom behind the chapel
The constant wind stopped, our napkins settled down
We blew across our coffee cups
It was over and no one had to say so

Reina Rosa has a prodigious memory. Her souvenirs go back to before she was born. What she remembers cannot be denied -- the hot llano, the swaying mesquite, dirt floor, smoke, buzzing flies. Abuelita, long dead, frying garlic with fideo in the afternoon, knew this. She said once,"Quit this preoccupation with the past, there's no future in it; your hermana is too far away, gambling in Nevada, to slap you out of your sueño.

Pocho Deer Song
After the Yaqui tradition

El Venado says: you, who do not have
Enchanted legs, what are you looking for?

Que buscas? Hear me, I say:
I am the pocho alive in the wilderness, and I tell you
Poetry is as extraordinary as eating tortillas in the kitchen.

One of the deadly sins is being *ordinario.*
We are not ordinary.
Haven't we deformed the national electorate? Haven't we
By sweat and cunning tweaked the national mercado?
Don't we have numerous prestigious think tanks?

Remember:
Chew roses before you write your poems.
Let your friends devour you, make yourself their banquet.
Each lie, alive in the dark is forever young.

Remember:
Writing is an intensified accident.
You never really know the answer, you die without knowing.
If you have to know, don't ask.

Like anyone else I require:
    Brisas suaves
A little bubbly
Ecstasy
Is it true you often think only because you feel?
Isn't the first author of the world human feeling?
Is the impulse to suicide part of the literary instinct?

Speaking solely for myself:
I spy devils.
I fumigate my lecheries with *ceniza de piñon.*
I am sometimes poor.
I am soft, gentle, never self-assertive.
I can yelp like a dog.
I respond to classified ads.

I am the Pocho alive in the semi-wilderness.
Shall I not become a free loan association for La Raza?
Shall I not greet a man without paying 6% for the effort?
Don't we become beautiful when we love the unseeable?
Will the whirlygigs sing again in the Mayan evenings of my mind?

I am the Pocho alive in the virtual wilderness.
I have spilled myself before the dawn.
There are yet noons and dusks to be splashed.

I am the Pocho alive in the fantastic wilderness.
Sometimes I sprinkle *cominos* over myself.
But even then, as I am walking out the door,
I am still the same flavor.

El Venado says: It used to be much better
But it is still going on, the wilderness still listens,
Listens to itself – even now.

I am the Pocho alive in the semi-wilderness.
Shall I not become a free loan association for La Raza?
Shall I not greet a man without paying 6% for the effort?
Don't we become beautiful when we love the unseeable?
Will the whirlygigs sing again in the Mayan evenings of my mind?

I am the Pocho alive in the virtual wilderness.
I have spilled myself before the dawn.
There are yet noons and dusks to be splashed.

I am the Pocho alive in the fantastic wilderness.
Sometimes I sprinkle *cominos* over myself.
But even then, as I am walking out the door,
I am still the same flavor.

El Venado says: It used to be much better
But it is still going on, the wilderness still listens,
Listens to itself – even now.

Garcia names one dog amor and the other es perro. Both are the barking chihuahuas of his heart. I am the god of the immediate vicinity, he says. In the sand mural he paints with egg tempera. Chavela, his consort, looks like Frida with freckles. She wears a reboso, embroiders brilliant scenes on scraps of typing paper. In the morning they moan and roll and drink coffee in bed. Tonight they call the dogs to feed on old menudo. "Venganse mis animas," G shouts into the arroyo, dripping paint into the sand.

A saguaro with charisma next to the gas meter and high voltage line. Garcia's head, full of name brands, antacids, year-end sales, thirst quenchers, tries to imagine the desert he is lost in. Other cacti blow their vibes, keeping him awake with anticipation as he kicks back in the yard. Nopal onda synapsia crackle and pop his angle of repose.

Garcia's Walking Pharmacopaeia Blues

I am a treatment resistant self-medicator.
I am my own pharmacopaeia of *medicinas*.
I produce therapeutic *drogas* at no cost to myself.
Lycozymes in my tears, antibodies, deadly interferon
Viral headhunters, lymphocytes & polymorphonuclear
Leucocytes, massive hordes of immunoglobulin and
Marauding T-Cells swim in my blood like Navy Seals.
Swirling in my medula: endorphins, enkaphalin, dynorphin
L-Dopa, Testosterone.

This treatment-resistant *auto-medicador*
Doesn't care if the major pharmaceuticals can
"Drill down to the needy patient anywhere in the country."
The barking chihuahua of my heart continually wards off
The evil eye. I don't need a depression pocket alarm card,
A Zoloft slide kit, or the Prescription Drug User Fee Act of 1992.
Nobody messes with my seratonin re-uptake pump.

My metphysical *angostia* is none of Pfizer, Lily, or Merk's *negocio*
How do they know when I've suffered enough?
There really is no pill for suffering. Agony doesn't
Recognize pills. Pills don't explain the justification
For grief. Can suffering come to an end within my point of view?
Do we meet somewhere in infinity if we take our separate
Views of agony far enough?

I, the long term chronic treatment resister,
Ignore the corporate Narcs. Take a look:
Norpramin
Indiral

Norpramin
Norpramin w/Indiral (to counteract doubt)
Prozac
Yocon

Prozac, Norpramin & Yocon (to counteract priapism)
Wellbutrin
Tenormin
Zoloft (Zoloft w/Tenormin & Norpramin to counteract ridicule)
Desyrel
Buspar
Lithium(Lithium, Buspar & and a handful of dirt to counteract drift)
Paxil(Paxil, Lithium & Acidophilus for stomachache)
Pondamin with Paxil (because Paxil makes you eat like a pig)
Synthroid (Paxil with Synthroid to climb mountains)
Surzone
Luvox (Luvox w/ Surzone to shield the eyes from shame)

I am the treatment resistant prince of pain.
Believe me, *la metaphore del dolore,*
Firmly confronted, transforms the *Cuerpo of Tristeza,*
Molds character and illuminates the muse.
Pain transfigured has the face of the muse,
The face with which we fall in love.

Yucca in moonlight -- a thousand lips glisten with silvery lust, unspoken, unquenched. There is no consolation, it seems, only light on the thick stalk -- veined, fleshy, phallic. All Garcia can be is voyeur, hoping for a glimpse of midnight llano agave conception.

G, anchored by fascination, thinks: nothing surveiled, nothing voyeured. His poise, a prairie dog's under pale stars, for a peek at the unviewable – sex with the moon! Silvery genome exchange! Waiting between moon and blossom agave stiffened lunar viagra yearning for release.

Menudo

Reina Rosa wears crimson camisas
She says "Curioso, es la piel
The skin that connects us --
Mira, tu my stiff upper lip."
Agua caliente sound propulsion
Fork plunge tunes meat
Vapor caliente makes for vistas maravillosas
Isla del Muerto cebolla cilantro
Hot tripe I love you so

The taste is in the skin
Hands drip red chile
Tongue wags chile red
Alone in the kitchen with me
"Curioso, tequila breath," she says,
"Menudo tripas roll and boil
Aire de vapor the taste is in the skin
All taste, all tiempo, orale
Its agua its gas its heat its time
Chile time red time skin time entero
Meat time diminished to a seventh
To a low flame to a slow flame fierro lento
Manny Fierro con cuchillo ala luna
It's cooking time that connects us
Time to get it get back across
La linea la migra la frontera de vapor.

It's que pasa when you smoke too many frajos
Your skin is smoked like chile like sex
Huele de humo huele de chile huele ahumada
The taste is in the skin."

"Curioso," smoky Reina says, "es como
Getting old and never getting young
Never otra vez again
Taste disappears sabor desaparecido
In dichos ahumadas. Ramon!" She says,
"hay animales en ti"

There are animals in you,
Snake Coyote probably Tortuga
Y Toro & zorro, yes zorro y zorillo
Plus tequila and deposits of nitro
In the meat that connects us."

"Curioso, down by the Rio wings
Wings play the banks *a bajo*
Down there for me cool my wet breast
Down by the Rio far from the kitchen
Abajo by barrancas herons and golondrinas
By orillas verdes green banks
Wet breast and golden sol formar
Pequenas ondas ripple
Rizar el espejo del agua

"Curioso wash your days in Rio water
Curioso, it's the heart that connects us
Curioso, remember birds want to feed on your heart
Remember you are the cry in the smoke
The smoke in my heart the taste in my skin."

Regador

Pulling a boot from the muck I curse my gods,
My shovel, the field of *maiz* going dry,
The *acequia* running slow, the sun way up.
Pushing water all morning into cracked earth
Sweat beads my arms and face, the shovelhead
Is heavy with mud and I am feeling old.
But the field's quiet rustling soothes my crusted
Self with clean silence as it drinks deep.
And I also drink something in that acre
Of bent praying tassels full of bees
Humming to their gods and mine, and shuffling sideways,
Apologize to a few felled stalks,
Their small arms wilting in the path
Of the advancing water bead, scrape
Thistle and bindweed with sharp *azadon*
In the dusty cool furrows, mutter to green
Clenched green fingers of corn root
As they drink, still alive by my sweat and care,
Inform them out in the middle of their humming field
That soon I will devoutly cut out and consume
Their pure, milky hearts and burn their remains
While humming to their gods and mine.

Tencha measures out handfuls of niztamal. Chuparosas hum and thrum in the garden, watching her cook. A neat pile of fresh hearts darken imperceptibly by the horno. She preps her shiny obsidian for mincing.

Out by the jacuzzi, Garcia sees the Corn Goddess braiding her hair, humming a sacrificial tune.

Cook up some pork chops for no reason, sing a song, swallow some passing clouds

I

I'm hardwired for death (I say to myself)
and speculate on the fringes of chaos,
cook up some pork chops for no reason,
sing a song, swallow some passing clouds.
I am suddenly cunning. And on the other hand,
others so easily manipulate me,
say a child or a bird. Children will be
drawn to me – for instance by my
sitting in a chair and smiling gently.
For the child, I should say,
(here I have a quizzical look in my eyes)
understands me. Small birds want
to feed on my heart, I know it.
I worry about them as the trees turn gold.

II
Imagine that, a man like me watching
The moon all night, night after night.
The same moon and the same stars
Or a satellite like the one moving south-
To-north through the realm. Really, south-
To-north, oddly, because of our human need.
Or, like a rolling ball on wide curves
Through prairie towns when I was driving once
All night, and said to myself while summoning Orion
Out of the ground in whispers (c'mon, c'mon)
I like to catch the moon sliding sideways
Through the rearview and out the window, like
Last week on an all night drive through Oklahoma
With Peaches asleep on the passenger side, I watched
The stubbled silvery fields passing and said
To her: I want you to speak again in your sleep
As I do when the moon, like a yellow coin, sets.

Reina's poem about walking Hwy 518 on a windy day in el taconito, drinking tequila, passed by whizzing cars, the neighbor dogs chasing them for kicks, the coke whore she was secretly in love with driving by with her adolescent lover.

She has abandoned her daughter. She will betray herself. She has only a gram or two left in her tiny purse . . and the frilly socks raised behind her ears in the dim adobe room . . . like flower flesh, virgin, first pressed . . . because of the pendejo father.

Death of a Soldier

Inadequate son, faulty pupil, he
Will have died for peace.
So much will have depended on it
We know what kind of capers he cut
How he used to parade in his underwear
Making faces in the mirror – pig noses
For junior, Chinese eyes, that kind of thing
      The new dead are husks, they are incubates
Is it possible to locate? The value, I mean,
Of indifferent army men sitting in the attic
Introspecting which dreams lead where,
Of the great arroyo, so clean, but collecting flotsam
On the fringes. (We know who dumps there at midnight
Their plate numbers)
      The new dead are remainders, they are changelings
Dupe of more worldly others, he will have seen them
Over the Rio, Mars and Venus triangulating the moon.
It will have given him *scalos frios,*
He will have counted to zero and kept on going,
The spit-shined sergeant attending the altar
      The new dead are casings, they are virtually essence
Talking of peace come from tatters of the old
He will have finally looked it in the face
Tentative, lamb-like, tilting on tiny hooves
Profanity treading night's veiled pubis
Confident of its dark fecundity
      The new dead are skins, they are tadpoles
He will not have interviewed well
The beginning is over, of course, its nebula a billion ends
Condensing infinity. The arroyo disappears in spectacular dust
One expression will have been vacuous, dreamy
Casual, utterly indifferent. He will have kept that image
In mind as jets streak sky flecked with cloud
      The new dead will dillydally, they are hatchlings

Dear Reina, I apologize for being false, weak, old. This morning I enraged my son, who doesn't speak or hear my tongue, when I said I wanted more communication. He wants to grasp the informal juxtaposition, the life bite, pen the saga of filial intrigue. It's almost noon, and he's been gone for years. His girl makes him dinner, wears tight jeans, and has a 4.3 average, the only woman on the team. Father and son, without us there'd only be the cars passing on the highway, the birds nesting in the eaves, the lonely moms.

Garcia was raised to give his blood. At the age of 10 he was introduced by his father on national TV as a future suicide bomber for humanity. Going down for God. His pen was the verdad barrio Sal Si Puedes.

Song X

After thirty years in the business the topic of song
Is car speed, and whether we're in the mood
      The mountain has a voice
      An invisible word we listen for
      Caught between summit and abyss
      We prick up our ears
What I really need is self-imposed virtual solitude
So that I need not take long walks at dawn with people
I've only met over the phone
      The wind has a song
      A woven aria we mentally
      Applaud while polishing ourselves
      Doing up our lips in the mirror
After 60 years of driving way above the speed limit
My passengers mean for me to increase my speed
I tell them: assimilation can occur at any velocity
It can be utterly destructive very close to home
I tell them: if you want to change speeds
First change your criteria. Your criteria for youth
That has escaped. Your criteria for *payaso* venue.
Your criteria for bureaucrat become musician.
      The cactus has a heart
      A succulent fist we dig for while lost
      In the panhandle searching for Pa
Precursors to song x gave us:
      A face in the water
      One star at dusk
      Bats flitting through the bosque
At 90 the mind casts off, forgets
Whatever it wants, remembers spontaneous remorse
At heel-crushing a wasp.
      Dazzling diaphanous
      Orange sky
      Ruined wings

Casino

I'm about to hit the roulette table
Between the dollar slots and the poker salon
This gives me some pace and intent
I've had my wine so I sit and choose red
Swaying in my chair I hear my red heart
Clicking black black black black black
As the dealer pumps the ball around the wheel
Some of this dark gets inside my head
Sense comes to my cortex – a blue sense
At the end of the day's run of syllogism
And the coming night lacquers the windows
Beaded with the lights of the dreaming city
And the dealer finally sees my hundred, smiles
And says Dollars? I say Dollars! He says Good luck!
I need it. Everything I'm wearing is donated – Hawaiian
Shirt, duck pants, Nikes. My car is donated
And needs a quart of oil to go 50 miles.
I need my teeth fixed and must piss every
Forty-five minutes, my dinner was ramen with old
Squash and sixty bucks would bring me even with my losses
Good luck I whisper to myself Red Red
I say to the wheel out loud Come On Red!
Bing bong bingditty bing bong bong bong ding
And the ball rolls past red 9
And rolls past red 16 and red 35
To that obsidian chip off the old abyss

Reina's charisma increases with her visibility and men gladly, hungrily, do her bidding. Discretion, a form of prudence, is a whim to her. Designers are eager to contribute props, photographers and video crews document her exploits, and these images are the commodity she markets to collectors – a demented form of moji perfunctionism. Reproduction glamorizes her experience and leaches it of ambiguity & emotion. Out of context, she's not sexy at all. She's about shame —of the observer, of the observed, of the portrayed. Feet, and the acquisition of shoes, obsess her, a lonely bruja doing an impersonation of Venus, possessing no imagination for ordinary happiness. Binging on sex tantalizes her with a fleeting taste of infinity -- assembling a frame for its emptiness.

Day of the Dead

Early Friday evening she phoned, "Let's
Drive down to the end of the road." And I
Said, "Yeah, and take a six pack and smokes
Park and kick back." So I went for the beer
And picked her up on the way.

When we got there it was sundown on the mountain.
The aspens were back lit as if by searchlights.
And that's when I thought, "What if there was a crowd
Of people we knew there behind the leaves trembling
With rays and their cars and they hollered out to us
(Like Mandy & Ramon, who were dead, would have)
"Come on, bring your beer!" So I told her that
And she began looking at the flaming gold leaves
Too, and said, "Yeah, what if all our friends
Were there, even Mandy & Ramon."
And her hand went to her mouth and we looked at each other.
The thought was mutual. She looked at the ignition key
Until I turned it, hung a U and took off.
We drank the rest of the beer back at the house.

"Arid serenity around the idea of spirit," Garcia says to himself. " The Sonoran desert's terrestrial swell, fluttering shadows, dark arroyos moist as devil's food."

Captive of all he wishes to contain, Garcia, the most hollow soul, turns his inside out. Starved for spirit, he comforts himself with a landscape whose perfect wholeness will satisfy him once and for all – a totalitarian future of infinite recomposition.

In the quiet afternoon by the swimming pool a shy young wetback from Yucatan turns off his roaring leaf blower and tells Reina his name. Oiled and tanned, bikinied and reclined, she asks him later, under magenta clouds, "Do you have a place to go?"

He cannot answer her.

Soon, they turn their backs on the glassy water and drift to the cool grass and oleanders. There her suggestions, one by one, bring his dead tongue to life.

Nogal

I was formed in the arroyo
But the mesa is where I live.
I pierce myself with barbed
Pencas from the canyon, the ones
Granpo never paid attention to.
Kneeling in mica drift
These frizzed *canas* of nogal
Whisper by the rio:
    Way too cool
    You wired and stamping fool
    All your life: cerveza, cerveza, cerveza
      ajo, ajo, ajo
    Way too cool for your own good
    Way different
    You're a greasy hairball in orbit
    You wired and dancing *pendejo*
Through chokecherry and wild plum
Beveled with dew, I,
The one named for forgetting,
Recite the name of each
Blade of grass whipped in the wind.

Climb the canyon, *domecilio*
Of gravel and grain where
It's easy to remember exactly
Those nogal whispers:
    Way too cool, natural
    Too cool for your own good
    Way too beautiful for you
    Get lost

Winter Dance

After Horace iii, 28

What could be better on an off-Sunday in winter?
Blackie, put on the ribbon shirt and feather
Let the dancers pound Mohawk while the sun blazes.

Your shadow living stone adobe while
Ben and Robert turn and flash the plains —
Going low and blowing smoke.

I'll attend quietly on snowy straw, humming
Bass from the throat, soprano from singing heart
Fringed maidens stepping through furred leathermen

After Easter I'll reply with Yaquil
Wirikuta hunting chants, deer chant
Then the song to Guadalupe

Moon queen and how she reigns, leading
The flower people through shadowlands
Carried on lunar horns.
Then a song to the sun's flowing blood.

Hand Dance

It's a dance that commemorates an ancient happening.
In a great circle she moves with her hands outstretched.
The mountain in the distance is blue with white streaks.
A fat crimson bow sits in the hair on her neck.
We must be attentive when she sidles nearby,
Her iridescent feathers shimmering before us.
A glint of sun flashes from her earring.
Her pursed lips make a tiny bow.
In the breeze under her downcast eyes
A fringed shawl of magenta on her arm
Sways to muffled drums where clouds hover.

Whirling Disease

Lover of icy streams with your arms sunk
To the elbows. I cast a loop at a rising.
In the last shards of streamlight you fling
A rainbow up on the *orilla* with both hands.
The flat green mirror rotates my waist
Over gravel shoals from last summer.
There's no one else in the gorge and red willows
Whisper so. Afternoon engraves late shadows
Turns tail and swims away down the escarpment.

Horse Eats Man

On the first night of our camping trip
Bernal got so shitfaced he couldn't stand.
Suddenly he got up, whooped and threw some bullets
Into the fire. We ducked and scattered pronto.
Still standing after they went off, he ran to his horse
Put a foot in the stirrup and leaped up and over
Into the bushes on the other side, whoomph.
He jumped back on without looking at us laughing and took off.
We hollered into the night for him to come back.
Later some wet hooves appeared near the fire
And a stranger from upstream said, "What's all the commotion?"
In the morning we searched and found his staked horse
Had eaten all the grass in a circle around
Where Bernal had slept there was only matted grass
In the shape of a man. We never saw him again.

A sweating illegal from Xalisco pretends to drink a long cool one in the empty rail car. The coyote who took his boleto waves goodbye from the façade of the vacant theme park.

Ah, the border and its inch-deep river, the sizzling rails, the patrols in federal brocade, the pistolas loaded with humanitarian bullets.

Part Four

El Mirador

The talking stick pauses mid-sentence, leans this way and that in the breeze from the bay, and begins again. "The yucca are in bloom," she says. "They, like me, are in love with the moon, pale crescent poised aside Venus in the blue."

Garcia clears his throat to answer her. It is so noisy in his head he must force thought to his tongue, so he hears nothing of what she says next, so preciously, swaying this way and that in the quiet breeze.

The View From Here

Reach down below the subflooring
Turn off the main valve to the whole house

    Shadow is concrete, a mist capable of *oscuro*

Behind yellow bulbs and passing crowds
On the sidewalks of Paseo Pueblo Sur
Hips and breasts of La Reina Rosa beckon

    The shadow is contained in the ray.

Llano is revealed yard by yard
Sun climbs the ridge

    Without light there is no shadow

Can you really fix anything?
Can you fix my leaking faucet?
Can you fix my creaking back?

    The shadow as well is spoken by the sun.

At the end of the day across the street
My silhouette bobs across golden fence boards

    Reason requires a subject between the sun and me

Drop the back of your head to view
Final play of yellowfuchsia rays in high cloud

    The sun is an instrument of psychodrama

Coastal peaks flash neon
In a dusk blood flameout
At the El Mirador Motel

    Extract from the light its shadow

Giant Screen

She comes over
I've got the giant screen on
In the blue glow she says
Put on the movie with Tupac
The one where he dies, her ankle
Arcs whenever he's on
I watch her watch the movie

Another one over for the evening
Says put on that Bogart movie
The one where he's a rich American
With a smoking jacket in a room in Italy
With Gina Lola and what's her name
I watch her watch the movie
Her ankle arcs whenever he's on

Little Sophie, over for the weekend,
Her five-year-old voice asks
Can I please see the Messican movie
I slip a '36 Pedro Infante in the slot
The blue glow disappears with her small sighs
As Pedro sings Immaculate Male in Guadalajara
I watch her watch the movie

From the unlit corner of not knowing
Each feminine profile a sculpture of whispers
To a lover who cannot hear
A shape with the value of truth
A waking dream empty of this but full of that
I watch them watch the movie

Menopause Motel

Curve of the hip
Flash in the curve
Whooshing sound
Of heat in the head
Orange blue light
Sunk in hot sheets
At a point in life
Driven the Black Range
Crossed the hot street
Broken the hot dream
Hotter than vacant
Unseen coyotes, Yes,
Hear them? Yes
Lift the covers to cool
Face and shoulder become
Spirit matters
Facets of sequence
Reasons electric arrive
With flame's tap on the shoulder
Did you know
The *Ojo* Snail's
Heated color
Foretells the sun's lash
On Cerro Azul
On dry roadkill smiles
On your brow turning
Upward in pale dawn
Shedding that hot sleep

Pretending it's accurate, Garcia's coyote gives him a bad map, sends him north across the border, tells him to move along prontito. Soon G is lost in the underbrush. "This must be the panhandle," Rosa's red lips whisper from behind him. "My coyote gave me the same jodido direccion," she hisses. "Que barbaro el chingado leaving us out here like this!" A part of G is secretly happy. For all he knows, he could spend eternity out here with her in el taconito.

Principle of the Moon

Cold moist feebly shining dark
Feminine corporeal passive
The lover the womanly and gentle
Sister bride mother spouse
Confab of beloved and lover
Embrace the 28th day
Vessel of sun universal
infundibulum terrae
take in and pour out heaven
take in sunlight sidle up
extract from him the molten seed
earthen born silver soaks up stars for gold
the bride conceives like whitest snow
the shine chases away the rabid dog
saving the divine child *umbra solis*
house of horn muse of dew juice
sap tears sweat blood vapor spit
grace is the principle wizard's liquor
aqua mirifica purifies flesh for soul
circle tree root metal aeon
silence in incomprehensible air
wafts me on its belly sphere
If you slay me you will understand

Reina Rosa was painting things the way she wanted them to be. There was the omega draped in peach damask. It was either an ending draped in beginnings, or a conception draped in obsidian. Whatever, it had great dark eyes. The bonsai on her banco had been hit by her gaze. Its branches were tubular rubies humming the key of D. It was all very luminoso, even when it upturned its dun-green leaves.

Reina Rosa seeks transformation ala brava, dreams Cheech & Chong reruns. Wow, que tightly wrapped dreams! Dreamt last night she killed a man, stripped him, and left him in an elevator. Reina, naked, went down a hallway in a trench coat, red hat, high heels, & lots of makeup. It's Reina taking over as CSI with a chicana sneer! Reina dreamt questions for the dead man in the corner, all the time thinking, "Go low, show low with mom and cuzins, going low and blowing smoke, the holy sacrifice of the que sufrisimo. Lay the weenie on the altar of sacrifice and chinga el crime scene investigator! Lowride lo show with mom and preems! Hecha le compañera Rosa!" Wakes up tightly wrapped in her sheets thinking, What questions? Awake, she asks herself, "Will that be my legacy? Lowride lo show with mom and primos? Crime scene investigator? Questions for the dead man in the corner? Mi jacalito covers my head (place to cook my beans, sleep, and dream of mi tierra.) Wakes up tightly wrapped in her sheets thinking, What questions? Going low and blowing smoke, lowride lo show with mom and the preems? Reina taking notes in the corner.

The Love of Garcia

Outside it is cold
But just inside the door
As soon as Garcia
Comes in at night
He finds his love
Not the love of Marquez
Not the love of Sandoval
But his love
Suitable to his soul
Not boundless
Nor light-filled
Nor causing ecstasy
Maybe once....
 Pleasurable as a private blush
Interesting as a fantasy
A halo once engulfing him
It is now smaller than his head
And getting smaller

In the kitchen
He plays with it
In the wooden bowl
Like a beautiful salad

He is careful to keep
The doors shut, the house warm
He is certain today
Or maybe next week
It will start to disappear
Become a small dot
Smaller than a pinpoint
Hard to find

Garcia atop the hill of the rooster crowing, "We have run for our lives and made it across alabrava with Candelario leading the way." G crows every morning atop another hill, like Sisyphus in the desert except for the shopping malls and security guards and gated communities. The gatehouse cop smiles derisively and tells him to turn around and enter the back way. "Don't think this is gonna be any better than el taconito or Tijuana," says Candelario before he throws it in reverse.

The young Tapatio in Levi's is lying in the cargo container. The agent is looking sideways. The CSI is kneeling, rubber gloved, at his swollen feet, touching an ankle like a ripe tomato. The sky is pale above the rail yard and roads spread out like hot spokes in every direction.

My Cemetery

Sun that glitters off the sea,
He thinks. The sign always says
No Admittance. Absurdly prominent
Verdance. Fuchsia, bougainvillea, old rails
By the parking lot empty of 1,000 cars.

Concept of a smile in mind.
Idea and smile surround
Full lawns with headstones.
Each step and the sign before it
Become a constant masque.

Oxidizing bronze is a green idea.
Marble antiques, chrysanthemum,
A dazzled walk on iron tracks
Sheened with heat pleads no contest.

Afternoon breeze, cypress shadows
On this tanned geezer sauntering
Among graves with small butterflies
Nailed in light and yellow forever.

The glitter, the absurd, the breeze, the idea:

Magenta blossoms in cedar verdichrome
Patina conceal in pungent scent the sign's command.

Traveling Circus in Española

So I get dressed and go, unthinking
Elephants prance in someone else's dream
This forgetfulness, this care for strangers
Gets me into so much trouble…

So I get dressed and go, unthinking
I have no room for any more love
Yet it comes
The last heart note of the day
Falls to the juggler's feet
 I couldn't agree more…

So I'm dressed and I go thinking
Distance, trapeze, and sequins
Bring new sense to old utterance
Just take what the day gives
Don't rage at the tyranny of choice…

So I've dressed and gone thinking
The carny man barking prices
The shivering toy poodle under his arm
Remind me: what takes place is a permanent declension
What we have constructed falls away…

So I'm dressed and I'm gone
A Chaco wind is whipping the mesa
Scintilla flash of flying acrobats
Whirls me in the air with angels singing
And I see far into Mexico…

So I've gone and I'm going
The tent ropes whirr on eyebolts
Frightening the dusty zebra
The pygmy Rhino measures the bars
Shuffling indigo dusk
Above the escarpment…

So I'm ready to leave
Laughing crowds under the big top
As the trick rider flops
A caricature of saddled seriousness
In which I am so earnestly bent

The sonso kept a sand and rock garden. There was no fence, no gate. His rake had only two teeth. The sand threw concentric shadows around the rocks in the slant light.

"I never have to water," said the retardado, "just rake and shove." The alabaster Buddha looked across the scene, tranquil amid the graffiti (!ftroop siempreconsafosese!) sprayed by homeys in metallic black across his nicho.

Astronomer Garcia

The plain is cloth spread out
Under a winter sky
On a frayed ribbon of road
I'm draped on a fence humming
Threads of an old tune:
La puerta musicale

You can't tell or ask,
But you can guess how
Equations flex in Astronomer
Garcia's skull when he turns
The wheel toward home at the barbed
Wire of inequalities
Blossoming into notes of an idea

Where does it arise this connecting
Something with nothing this noise
In the pipe of habit this number
In space from which we spring

The mind pries the prairie's mask
Reveals stone, exposes
Angel bustle plumes
In nogal and arroyo, alien
Landscape familiar and dear

High cloud yodeling
Pure sky songs
Earth holds their maelstrom
Steel radials erode
In solar *rayos* penetrating
The logic of syntax finding
A way to metaphor tomorrow
And today is a small tomorrow
Small tomorrows are OK

Expression Three

Control your own experiment, study
The manual on how to build the machine
That builds the machine, the machine that runs
On something else, the random amid bursts
Of sinister, of sense, the machine that makes the book
That writes horizon's true line and radiant
Serifs among leaves of silhouette oak
Reverse transcript of common utterance
Return ticket to *llano de nada ningun*
Whose paragraphs are lines of blue chamiso
Where ancient malediction's muscled hulk
Stalks below the blossom line
For every pounce a mouthful of *maligno*
Prowls the light dream edge of word
Puppet of recognition, reverb without *lengua*
Endlessly with a selfish purpose:
Disentangling fact from fabrication
Questions from products of a story line
Whose relation to the point is coincidental
Capable of ruining a page that stays the same
No matter who you become or where you are

Coyotes! Carnales! Two with condemned eyes take my money and measure my stamina through the fence in Calexico. They are far too young and track-suited to be simply coyotes. Xylar, spandex, Nike and nylon – must be narco-coyotes!

Over the chain links, high stars offer guidance via sparkling spears. G, silent, on the US side with his net bag and his 3x5 card with direccion. There is the immense billowing of sagebrush and creosote, the ridiculously narrow path, the invisible horizon, and the faint sound of weeping.

Garcia Walks

I've been walking for a thousand miles
I walk and walk and walk
The schemes I've walked through
      mechanized agriculture
      nuclear missiles
      suffering Madonna
      November 22nd
      Government Protection
      Spinning black holes
      Cold fusion tubes
      Black Monday
      Liars Poker
      Chaos Theory
      The War on Drugs
Same sidewalks same streets same dogs same schemes
Different cities different states different names
I'm walking through a curtain of schemes
Each fold each pleat a silky obstacle
Whenever I see a scheme I walk right into it
I cheerfully walk through schemes
      Scheme of full employment
      Scheme of the rotary engine
      Scheme of the 900 number
      Scheme of solar energy
      Scheme of wind power
      Scheme of total connection
Impressive such simple schemes
I love walking through them steaming greening misting darkening
What could happen to me as long as I keep walking
      Walk away from it all
      Walk into everything at once
      Walk with an angel bustle
      Walk for health and fitness
      Walk into a hall of mirrors for a course correction
      Walk away from myself
Is it someone (No! It's me!)
Walking into another scheme
If I stop walking will it be time to figure
Which was the most impressive?
Oh shut up and keep walking

"If ya gotta know, don't ask." Garcia has left an entire saga untold only to find the audience eager for a sequel. "When in doubt, head north," was G's idea of survival, even though his brother never returned from there. Still, G gets work everyday, washes up in the irrigation ditch, buys a loteria at the 7-11 each night.

G is working the melons in Colorado. Dreaming blue-grey agave of Jalisco explain the present he cannot understand. His mystery, a beautiful object of contemplation, keeps him from being tired. In the melon field, picked clean to the horizon, there is no answer anywhere to be found.

Garcia Builds a House

Try building a house
See what comes through the door
Before it's finished – first a dog
When the foundation is still wet
Sniffing the threshold.

Then a preacher telling me
I can be saved by the lord,
Jump start the trinity
Of wood, cement, and contractors
To bless my joists.

Then a lot of noise
About the cost of land,
Then a lot of rain
Slickening the 2x4s.

Whenever a cloud passes
Something else flies through,
Then the piercing stench of tar
Wafted as the roof is sealed,
Then a face in the frame smiling about
Something you know nothing of.

Reina inherited the right to tell the story. It circles her head as she crosses el puñonito at night. Her journey is a vision projected on the sand -- mesa, river, bosque. Before her, each black pebble is arranged, each bit of quartzite, each tuft of paja -- to form a unique landscape, an expanse of turquoise suffering pierced by golden joy surrounding the crimson fruit of the fire.

Garcia surrenders to his increasing blindness, an authentic and autonomous world, a dark paradoxical gift, a whole new order. Discarding his nostalgia for the visual, he finds a new onda. G reshapes his centro, jettisons visual memory from his dreams – loses the very idea of seeing. He resembles the mole, the worm, the nematode –
a number, a shape working through the dark.

Hombre in the Moon

I notice at midnight how an *arbol is* husky
With *bigotas*, big shoulders and silver-haired
When luna is high. Streaming shadows and winks
Of faded stars light the cheap plastic bowl
On the dusty sill full of the same light,
So grand. Que pasa? Silver mustache beards?
Laughing chaparral? Cracked luminous
Bowls? Bent shoulders? Indirect, secondary
Light, half missing, half there blinking for clarity

Dear Curioso, It's been a while since we shared the good times, the best of our piel, the mystery. I've been spending tiempo with another man. I've tried to be fiel to him, but, at various times, the least things remind me of you: the wide arroyo, new lettuce in the garden, anyone yodeling. Will we never be comfortable, our bones finally set, positioned, locked tight where we best could be? I love you with my sighs, my nalgas yearn for you. I don't know what else to say. Love is marvelous but it also brings pain. Like I'm not going to eat chocolate? I'm not going to hear the sunlight at midday with you, juicy man? Favor de sing me a song once in a while, bathe in the acequia madre when you think of me. And encuanto you're eating your frijoles, please taste me in el humo de la olla.

O piensas en mi.
Besos Y Abrazos fuertes, Reina

Real Experience

I experience a total rethink of
My previous existence as if all
The time before has been simply a set up
For this now. Then I think about
My skin, I had forgotten about my skin.

And why can't I find the restaurant I want
The one with the belly dancer gyrating continuously
Just out of the arc of sight, where
The waiter's linen arm flicks gracefully
Through fragrance, removing dead cigarettes?

A freak appearance, Juan, who always said,
I'm big, fat, and blind, peers from a photo
On the wall. I didn't know the point
Is to make your friends, make them from
Your own body of justifiable tristesse.

I didn't know my skin could feel so good
Remembering I haven't changed my mind
Still able to walk around, sense distorted,
Able to eat starches and greens, going
To all the attractions, forcing myself into
A state of emergency alert where I
Must rescue myself from introspection
Amidst uncomprehending condescension.

Emergencies avoided for years become moot.
I look within myself and hoot. I am
A voice that hears itself speak out,
A hand that grasps isolation like a witticism.
There isn't a part of me that doesn't get the point.

Inexplicably, I can't feel something
Bad is happening however I may feel
In the future. I dress myself
In clothes designed myself to restrain myself
From looking like others.

I take up my position as transient
Read a line from an homme d'affaires
Saying his name for me is *Now Under Construction*
And about tomorrow I should be proud
I say I'm afraid to be proud
It's my only virtue, I can't be part
Of some one else's movie
When I read him I am not me

Know I am not normal, I undermine it
With semi-faux self-appreciation
This is the dishonesty self-forgetting
Imposes on us before we die
There is solace in being web-caught sucked dry
I say to the spider as would a fly

Garcia considers himself a borderline concept. The glue of the world keeps him from peeling off the edge, along with an ongoing meditatio with the unseen – a gravitational relationship where the heaviest ideas emerge before his eyes -- an anchoring imaginatio.

This edifice of ideas becomes a cycle of material shape shifting – a syrup of the life forces. G the artifex, the indispensable condition of his own experiment, pours out subtle bodies with divine aspects. On the dry rim of the Arroyo Seco, he can see the air, uncorrupted, uncommonly light, has mind -- its heavy, solid kernel, a shadow, moves with it – a soul swallowed by matter.

Laughs

Your everyday laugh has a diminishing structure
Starting strong and ending soft
A laugh played backward sounds strange
Frightening, just as a reptile or a fish or an insect laugh
Might be frightening for a human

Because a laugh is more animal than talk
Yet still we know how human it is
A laugh on the playground is prehistoric
The way it blends in with the trees

Gather hundreds of episodes for evidence
Start with mundane experience
Laugh at your own statements
You must laugh first before others do

A man talking will laugh for response
The woman talking will laugh considerably more
The biggest laugh goes to the most appreciative listener
As when a woman speaks to a man with wit

The rules of laughing must be abided by
End your sentence before you laugh
Refract natural pauses in your speech
Don't laugh in the middle of someone's sentence
Don't laugh before your own sentence is finished
If you wish to be considered HA – HAHA – HAHAHA!
Normal

The lawfulness of laughter indicates
A segregation of the brain's processes
Speech and laughter, laughter and speech
We laugh and we speak, but never at the same time
We modulate our influence by assembling speech and laughs
Synchronize our moods and actions with laughs and speech

You could say we bark like dogs to coordinate
The disparate elements of thought mood and action
We form a blade of laughs to plow our way through the world

Laugh menacingly and flip the scale
Jeering malicious exclusive laughter makes a point
As you smash someone in the face

Laugh like a despot at the comedians
Dead on the gestapo's leash
Fashionable laughter requires tact

G's ritual in the carwash has little to do with the car. Not just a chopped '73 Mercury emerges gleaming in the sun, polished by sweating mojis. G pays extra for a spray of boiling carnauba wax – the clinging fire his soul craves. (Mystical purisima effects to bring him grace?) His eyes thus opened again to his imperfections, he looks about his landscape for a suitable sacrifice to seal his work at redemption.

Ordinary Pieces

He called me from "the set"
That's where he always wanted to be
The writer, whom everyone despises

South on Highland, hot
Looking for an iced drink
Pale memories sweat on each corner

There he is climbing the roof again
How many times will I
Send him up there for nothing

I waited so long for my revenge
And finally here it is at last
Regret enfolds me

I pack the gift carefully
With foam and bubble wrap, see again
Your blue curves under dawn windows

So what if the movie is overlong
So what if the star is only semi-nude
What do you want, movie insurance?

You say, "mimic the wilderness,"
And I laugh at the thought.
You mean get ready to disappear?

We drive down Camino Medio
Smoking, talking. It's good
To refuse condescending offers.

After the ceremony in a corner
Eyebrows plucked, dressed to kill, smoking.
There was aftermath, awkward in the shadows.

We suck, we do, everyone does.
Born sucking, grow up sucking, die sucking.
Hard to control, admit it. Feels good.

There was shimmy and vibe in the wheel
Rhythmic, modulated like a voice
That made him invent a song.

Constantia, obedienta, moderatio, aequalitas
All toward an image around midnight
Coming at him on the dividing line.

He waved off the ghost with his hand
Golden at the stumbling block
Frozen at the wellstone.

A lizard flicks in fits and starts
Again and again no sound
Exact, narrow awakening

Garcia's dead Mexican patron will not be replaced, nor will the giants who roamed la capital with him for so long. No other moji was addressed on equal terms with Plaz, Hortiz, Mandrade, Velez & Yarquez. His memory was the most psychedelic salon in the region. How he praised and reproached and inspired incipient G! This Viejo with obsidian eyes, belonging as he did to the inner circle... their last outing was when? Grifa's last opening at the galleria Bellas Artes? Preamble to the burning mattress? G should have questioned him before he died.

Part Fivr

Garcia in Gringolandia

Funebre en Amalia

Chasuble white linen with crimson cross
Alb and altar & Reina's candle freak out
Seeing no savior in the *capella*, just her swirl,
Swirling sin in the cold cielo lighting immense candles and
Padre's stitched crimson against her black pinstripes

Reina's steaming posole sopa and tamales sit in the *sala*
Delivered piping *caliente* to Los Hermanos who took the gig
Rosa's crimson lipstick glow under snowy eyelash as
La *familia* rolled in from outatown – San Luis, Cerro Gordo
Refinando in the victim's name, each later sinks in saliva

Working the funereal gig, she asks continual
Questions #1 thru #4: Created for non-eternal life?
Each death one piece of holy eternal? Each one
A holy fractal 3-D swirl mimicking eternal?
A swirl of Christian death in a larger maelstrom?

Reina celebrates the joy of the mass, the chapel's
Indirect lighting, blonde paneling wood swirls
Carved by Hermano Don Dionisio before her birth
Prepared to meet her Lord, all the angels
And saints? Do they stand with her now?

Through stained glass to Mt. Blanca snow cap
A million piñon and forty buffalo at *Cerro Cebolla*
Too many new homes near Mt. San Antonio
Thinking the new dead are remainders, they are chain gangs
Saying to herself: Forgive the sins of all these

Jammed into this *capella* including me! Reserve a place
In the kingdom! Thinking: Kingdom? Name of God?
Can the holy be a kingdom? Wood swirls, hymn swirls
In ice wind zero degree wind under Latir Peak
Strummed guitars bathed in the hum of sacrifice

Padre Jones, the sound of your gringo name pains me
Shimmering gold crucifix in her face shames me
Final accordion-polka procession with *santos* frames me
In the parking lot with Fermin & Squeaky after, a shot
Of tequila and some bitch weed to cool it down. Hey

Fermin and Squeaky! Take this all of you and eat me!
I give you my body -- my chichis my panocha
Take this and drink me! This, my alcoholic blood.
And smoke this *frajo entero* under ice clouds for luck!
Follow me and the coffin, *santos* swirling in my hair,

My magenta jacket lettering: *Sagrado Corazon de Jesus*
Fraternidad Piadosa de Nuestro Jesus Nazareno Dist. No. 3
Mascareñas Urraca Farm & Ranch, Inc., my muddy bootheels
And snowpatch on the way to la *cena funebre*
Do this in swirling mystery memory of me.

Dear G',

Pressing wholly on the ball side of the universe something fantastic keeps me on my toes. Duende hecha me bailar is my song. Spent Sunday in the Jemez with Cubans & Okies. Ah, que placer! Slow-baked on a propane fire, the apricot bars stuck to my lips, nuts worked around my tongue and kept my mouth too busy to sing. Time off, love, how rare and elegant next to a sparkling stream. Have been singing with the monsters and gaining air.
Pork roast and rice, E-packets and milk from a moon very close to earth on Wednesday -- un poquita de escalera y vamos. Yoga tonight with Sis -- standing on my head for hours. Even then can't turn my ears off now that I've had the CD biblioteca funk-shwayed. La la lalala la.

Amor, Luz y Pedasos
Reina

"Gardant un excellent souvenir du dejeuner avec toi lors de mon recent voyage au Seattle . . . " G considers his next line. The possibility of using the idea of solitude is exciting. But, venturing to the far side of isolation as an image projected by letter – inconsiderate and selfish. Perhaps "una noche hermosa de diciembre alla en la Habana . . ." or "Chica, dejame tocarte el wiwichu…" might be more familiar and simpatico, considering the divorce, the distance, the time elapsed.

San Ysidro 55

I
My mouth stuffed with tortilla stifling gritos
To match my uncles' (if I could) as guitarron
Plunge into La Negra drenched in spilled turtle blood
And small change we scramble for among whirling skirts
On the patio behind the bride and groom spiraling American
Far from Sinaloa how maniacal sus Mexicanos
In San Ysidro wedding sus chicharrones
Hide the rooster hill invisible chanclas
Chile aroma and tamale sus agua frescas
Soup de tortuga luz y lena sus bigotas mariachis
Black pantalones wool alive with silver buttons
Oh America baja con espaldas mojados
Wetbacks como su tacuches pinstripe cutaways
Swing with gold chains Jamaica tamarindo limo
Como they offer their sweat soaked weave
To be zapped by the sun old sol
Old padre burning copal to drain the clouds
And soak the maiz O Sinaloa
Su tequila is still made of agave heart cerveza mezcal
Out of those wetbacks who love me
I make a hacienda high above
The BofA its music unearthly
Wavers passing southward on jalapeno breeze
Blowing mariachi as heard in Xalisco once
This world made out of me and of them will stay
In America and die here while I go on making
Out of them that America started with a wedding

II
On a red patio pre-started with naked conception
Under eucalyptus trees and a moon pre-honeymoon
Not a mile from Tijuana what would all that
Tequila have made without what I have made of it
And the clouds rushing up from Mexico and through
And over the Baja Range their rain from the gulf
Tiburon and Penyasco echoes around this the deluge
Of blue from Sinaloa wet out of the arroyos wet happy
Wet exhausted wet like alambristas at last over the fence
The whole landscape changed by them their mestizo
Moji multi-truck farms suddenly strawberry
Iceberg Boston celery onion green
Green tomato luminosos themselves imagining
A west more west than their compelling million
Rows themselves an issue at land's end
Running like 1,000 thrummed book pages
At its end having changed a whole America
And the ocean breathes out evening at them in waves

Garcia In Gringolandia

Moreno from Dog Town
Grows to be a bato con orgullo
With an angle
Y seguro que hell yes the looks
Necessary to incite the imagination

Savvy dude from Dog Town
G has a nose for opportunity
Instinct drummed in by Jesuits
For challenge
Certain arrogance mirror rooms
      blue with smoke
Certain knowledge
      of what is necessary
Certain pitch for
      el cancion del final del mundo

There will be nodes of chaos
Where he will have
      no clue
A vortex of dollars in a realm
      of *rucas* in fufu tutus
Poems in the dark sung to *pendejos*
      concerned with outcomes
In the eternity between past and present
He assures himself daily of the angle
The angle he imagines is real
It will be the last to go

After 72 holes, one could say a physical slaying of Garcia's body had taken place. Sacred words of consecration were the sword. So, could he now deem himself a worthy location for the divine? Redeeming substance, freeing the captive soul? It is not G but the deity lost and sleeping in him revealed. The unknown substance is, of course, impossible to specify – root of itself, autonomous and dependent on nothing. True principium, uncreated, having nothing in common with the elements, lacking the visible string of qualities – hands, elbows, ears, hips, and an arcing fade to die for.

Garcia's *Luz* Especial

In a moonlit adobe Garcia revels
His thought-inflected Moji psyche
Refracts constellated luzlaluna
Turns hovering animas feministas
And the earth they observe to a nocturne
Perfect contrapunto to his solarity
Still, so lovely, directed inward though a frosted pane

Miles from any doctor, G increases
Intake of bearroot-angustifolia-tequila
Infusions as the round moon's light
Blends nocturnal shapes into unexpected unity

A newly comprehending Garcia
Says to himself: "Care nothing for
Discrimination, judgment, insight, turn
Your solar dark to the naked plenitude
Pulsing with your new special light"

Each refraction shifts in star-fade
G beneath dusty *vigas* without them
All stand for his enlightened self
Becoming his light though in truth he can't
Imagine what *luz* it truly is so plainly
Before him without mystery except perhaps
A sign for something else *mas elemental*
How it makes from the night a sign more
Than night containing more than light more
Than his own, more, even than itself

Garcia's Dog Poem

Dogs are not pets
      they are saviours
Gigantic dogs with pacific eyes
      guard my sheep
Tiny dogs with gigantic eyes
      piss on my tires
Let's get going and shear them for posterity
For the hair of the dogs will save us
Dog bones
      ground to a powder
            can save us
Pickled dog dick tacos
      save marriages
      by the hundreds
      in Korea
Black Dog
      ever vigilant
      redeemer servant
      lick my spotted shoes in the morning
White bitch
      pick Frisbees from blue sky
           with your teeth
RezDog blue with cold
      Watch me sleep
You are not pets you are party animals
      shaggy dogs not my children
      chieftains in a two foot world
      wear buzzard headdresses to a roadkill party
Noble-nosed hound sniffing rank corners
Lead me out of the dark

Let's eat one roasted in garlic
with Szechuan relish and cold beer

Dear Reina,

This is not a logical sophistry but a very real phenomenon of great practical importance, for it affects the problem of my identification in society. The highest value is safely embedded in matter, the starting point for science is granted, the conquest of death being its important by-product. Redeemed from mere materiality by our sacrifice, the nuclear reaction is one form of redemption.

Garcia Prepares For Winter

I
G crosses Pennsylvania
And the desert speaks to him
      from the cold stone of the Capitol
      from rush hour's traffic rage –
Speaks to him as his elders would
Each with the face of a frosted shrub
Closing the door behind him at night
Evening whispers needle his lobes
Sleepy G's dream at 3am:
      snakes out the door
      down the alley to the Potomac
      settles down in black sludge
Sleepy blue G sleepwalking:
      sinks in Anacostia backwater
      to terrapin level
      fetches it at sunrise
          horizontal
          certain
Softened
    pliable
G stakes it out like a skin
    to dry

II
Day clouds scud the billboards
Massachusetts signals red
      New Hampshire yellow
      Diamondback intersection swarm
A skull of ice
Pinned to the street sign
Shivers with his reflection
As he feels the winter bite

Dear Reina,

Intolerance and shortsightedness are to blame for my conflict with your faith. Following my masculine mind, I logically opposed a child of the earth to your child of heaven, and one of gems and metals to yours of sentiments and yearnings. Can you blame me for revealing my personal alchemical principles? The important thing is transformation. Even without it, I'll sooner or later have to pay the price.

Garcia's Rollergirl

Rollergirl all my life unendingly debut
while I sit in my convertible Dodge, my TV
Bean bag my movie seat waiting for you:
Tanya Denise Diane Jill Maria
To squeeze your toes in your roller shoes
And bump against my driver's side
Bruises and makeup in my face bustier
garter shorts tights mascara & speedos
Chippy of my mother's indignation
Venus of my first masculine independence
Rollergirl you endless psychic factor
Remain in your original form: bustier
Garters shorts tights mascara & speedos
Rolling through mind and finally morph into
Sacred whore unchanged for aeions
Spring of motive hot impulse & desire
Archaic form slamming hard my inner
Soul divine image of heart's possession

Garcia Meets The Holy Bitch

Insane pride and an idea
        in his head
Running down the arroyo
G follows her, nothing in his hand
Nothing in his pockets
        no offering?
Notes the magic in desire's cage
        and he presentless
        without even
        a ring
        a bracelet
        a talking stick
Yet he pursues her, catches up to her
        in self love?
        pupils dilated?
        hungering?
thinking as he approaches
        she never gives you everything
        very good very mysterioso her power
        does it stick to her ribs
        real, natural, Hershey Bar good
        how did she come about it
        did she ever lack the great quality
        what about the time truth first
        slid across her lips
        what licks she give and take
        what heroine's trek loaded her up with good
She turns throwing wide her SW trailer chic
        Kmart chemise de Chine
Keeps on the stretch pants and plastic sandals
        runs her hand up his loins
        presses his face to her breast
        breathes out her heat
        understands him always has
And G groans yes yes yes
Thinking
        this could be when you begin to sing

About the Author

Amalio Madueño lives in Taos, New Mexico. Long associated with the Taos Poetry Circus and Mexican Bob's Poetry Camp, he has published widely in journals across the United States and Europe. Recent anthologies featuring his work include **Venus in the Badlands** (ed. J. Macker, Santa Fe 2006) **The 315 Experiment** (ed. Dinsmore & Alley, Vancouver BC, 2006) and **Wandering Hermit Review** (Seattle, 2006). Upcoming work will be found in: **la Puerta, Taos the Art of Fetching Sky** (ed. antoinette claypoole, Wild Embers, Taos 2006), and **Muse6** (ed. L. Council El Paso, 2006). Amalio performs his work regularly throughout New Mexico and the west coast in featured readings, seminars, television & radio, as well as on videos and CDs.

Lost in the Chamiso is Amalio's first full-length book of poetry.

books by Wild Embers

Lost in the Chamiso
by Amalio Madueño

la Puerta, Taos the art of fetching Sky
anthology of artwork/interviews/poems
from/about Taos, N.M.

Rivers in Her Eyes
by antoinette nora claypoole

Coming in Spring 2007

Dreaming of True World
by Ed Little Crow, Dakota

Watershed Years
collection of interviews/stories about
the Peace House of Ashland, Or.

visit
www.wildembers.com
all People are One

www.ingramcontent.com/pod-product-compliance
Lightning Source LLC
Chambersburg PA
CBHW080444110426

42743CB00016B/3272